Chapters 1 & 5
Introduction to Law & Business Ethics

Chapter 1 and 5

Introduction to Law and Business Ethics

What is Law?

- Black's Law Dictionary defines law "…as that which must be obeyed and followed by citizens subject to sanctions or legal consequences; a body of rules of action or conduct prescribed by controlling authority, and having binding legal force."

Primary Functions of the Law

- Peacekeeping.

- Shaping Moral Standards.

- Checking Government Power.

- Facilitating Reasonable Expectations.

- Promoting Social Justice.

- Providing Stability and Predictability to Society.

- Protecting the Environment.

Flexibility

- The U.S. law is flexible.
  - The law evolves and changes along with the norms of society, technology, and growth and expansion of commerce in the U.S. and the world.

History of American Law

- Much of American law is based on the English law system.
  - All states except Louisiana base their legal systems primarily on the English common law.

History of American Law

- Courts of Law: empowered to award wronged parties economic compensation.
  - These remedies are: land, items of value, or money.
    - These remedies are called remedies at law.

History of American Law

- Courts of Equity: empowered to award any manner of non-monetary relief.
  - These remedies are: the injunction, specific performance, rescission, and reformation.
  - These remedies are called equitable remedies.

History of American Law

- Today, most courts of law and equity have merged.
  - Most U.S. courts permit the plaintiff (the suing party) to seek both law and equitable remedies against the defendant (the party being sued).

Sources of American Law

1. Constitutions.
2. Statutes.
3. Administrative Rules and Regulations.
4. Common Law.

Sources of American Law

- Constitutions set forth the fundamental rights of people living in the United States or a given state.

Sources of American Law

- The U.S. Constitution sets forth the structure of the federal government. The U.S. Constitution created the following three branches of government:
  - Legislative (Congress).
  - Executive (President).
  - Judicial (Courts).

Sources of American Law

- Statutes are rules and regulations put forth by legislatures.
  - Throughout the semester, we will encounter state statutes that were originally drafted as uniform acts. Uniform acts are model statutes drafted by lawyers and/or legal scholars.
    - Uniform acts do not become law until a state legislature enacts them.
    - Example: the Uniform Commercial Code (UCC) – includes laws and other regulations affecting commerce (bank deposits, warranties). These laws govern the different types of warranties that Microsoft, Toyota, and Sony provide with their products.

Sources of American Law

- When state legislatures delegate lawmaking authority to local government bodies, they are empowered to adopt ordinances.
  - Zoning ordinances, for example.

Sources of American Law

- Administrative Rules and Regulations. Administrative agencies are created by the legislative and executive branches of government. They may adopt rules and regulations that regulate the conduct of the covered parties.
  - The Occupational Safety and Health Administration (OSHA) oversees health and workplace safety and makes sure that workplace conditions are not hazardous.
  - The Environmental Protection Agency (EPA) enforces federal statutes in the area of environmental protection.
- Administrative agencies are often informally referred to as the "fourth branch" of government.

Sources of American Law

- Common law is law made and applied by judges as they decide cases not governed by statutes or other sources of law.

Hierarchy of American Law Sources

1. United States Constitution.
2. Federal statutory law.
3. State constitution.
4. State statutory law.
5. Administrative rules and rulings.
6. Common law.

The Doctrine of Stare Decisis

- This is a Latin phrase meaning to "stand on decided cases".

- Judges are obligated to follow precedents established within a particular jurisdiction.

The Doctrine of Stare Decisis

- This doctrine promotes uniformity of law within a jurisdiction, makes the court system more efficient, and makes the law more predictable for individuals and businesses.
- One of the most well-known cases associated with stare decisis is *Roe v. Wade*. This landmark case decided by the U.S. Supreme Court in 1973 made a decision on the issue of abortion. The Supreme Court decided that until a fetus is "viable," a woman may terminate her pregnancy for any reason. The Supreme Court went on to define viable as the ability of the fetus to live outside mother's womb, although with artificial aid. The precedent in *Roe v. Wade* still stands today.

Classification Systems of the Law

- Substantive Law and Procedural Law
  - Substantive law consists of laws that define, describe, regulate, and create legal rights and obligations.

  - Procedural law consists of all laws that establish and regulate the manner of enforcing the rights established by substantive law.

Classification Systems of the Law

- Civil Law and Criminal Law
  - Civil law defines and enforces the duties or obligations of private persons to one another.

  - Criminal law defines and enforces the obligations of persons to society as a whole.

Case Terminology: Parties

- Plaintiff: the party who filed a court action.

- Defendant: the party against whom the plaintiff filed its action.

- Appellant/Petitioner: the party challenging the trial court's disposition of the action.

- Appellee/Respondent: the other party to a disposition that has been appealed.

Case Terminology: Opinions

- Judgment: the court's disposition of an action.

- Opinion: the court's reasons for its judgment.

- Unanimous Opinion: an opinion joined by all of the judges who heard a case.

Case Terminology: Opinions

- Majority Opinion: an opinion joined by the majority (but not all) of the judges who heard a case.

- Concurring Opinion: an opinion by one or more judges who agree with the judgment of the majority, but not necessarily with its reasoning.

- Dissenting Opinion: an opinion by one or more judges who disagree with the judgment of the majority.

Business Ethics

- Law is a starting point or minimum for ethical behavior – just because something is legal doesn't mean it is ethical. And, sometimes the law may permit an act that is ethically wrong.
- Business ethics and business law are closely related because, ultimately, the law rests on social beliefs about right and wrong behavior in the business world.
- Most unethical business behavior occurs because management does not always make clear what ethical standards and behaviors are expected of the firm's employees.

Business Ethics

- Measuring ethics is personal: What one persons considers ethical another may consider unethical. There are, however, some universal theories about what conduct is ethical and what conduct is not. Two of those theories are: (1) Kant's Categorical Imperative and (2) Principle of Rights.

_____

_____

_____

_____

_____

_____

_____

Business Ethics

- Kant's Categorical Imperative: states that individuals should evaluate their actions in light of the consequences that would follow if everyone in society acted in the same way.

_____

_____

_____

_____

_____

_____

Business Ethics

- Principle of Rights: believe that a key factor in determining whether a business decision is ethical is how that decision affects the rights of others (such as, employees, consumers, suppliers).
  - A potential dilemma is that different stakeholders may disagree on what is most important to them.

_____

_____

_____

_____

_____

_____

Business Ethics

- The Foreign Corrupt Practices Act: was enacted for the purpose of making it unlawful for certain classes of persons and entities to make payments to foreign government officials to assist in obtaining or retaining business.
  - This addressed the saying "When in Rome do as the Romans do."

Chapter 2
Courts and Alternative Dispute Resolution

Chapter 2

Judicial Review, Jurisdiction, Courts, and Alternative Dispute Resolution

Judicial Review

- Definition: the process by which a court decides if (i) legislative enactments are constitutional and (ii) actions by the executive branch are constitutional.
  - Judicial review was established in the 1803 case of *Marbury v. Madison*.
    - Although this case was decided over two hundred years ago, it is still considered valid precedent. The federal courts regularly cite the case as a source of authority for the power to invalidate a law that conflicts with the U.S. Constitution.

Jurisdiction

- In order for a court to hear and decide a case, the court must have jurisdiction of the case.
- Jurisdiction is (1) about a plaintiff choosing the correct place to sue and choosing the correct court in that place and (2) about complying with rules of fairness for the defendant who will appear in court to defend her liberty or property.

Jurisdiction

- Jurisdiction requires a two-part analysis: a court must have both (1) subject matter jurisdiction and (2) personal jurisdiction.

Subject Matter Jurisdiction

- Subject Matter Jurisdiction is the court's power to hear certain kinds of cases. Subject matter jurisdiction determines which court system may hear a particular case.
  - Cases may fall under state jurisdiction, exclusive federal jurisdiction, or concurrent jurisdiction.

Subject Matter Jurisdiction: State Court

- The state court system has a broad range of jurisdiction.
  - State courts have the power to hear all cases not within the exclusive jurisdiction of the federal courts.
  - State courts also have exclusive jurisdiction over certain cases.

Subject Matter Jurisdiction: Federal Courts

- The federal court system has exclusive jurisdiction over very few cases.
  - Admiralty;
  - Bankruptcy;
  - Federal criminal prosecutions;
  - Lawsuits in which one state sues another state;
  - Claims against the United States; and
  - Cases involving federal copyrights, patents, or trademarks.

Subject Matter Jurisdiction: Concurrent Jurisdiction

- Federal Question: cases arising under the U.S. Constitution, federal statute or regulation, or a federal treaty.

Subject Matter Jurisdiction: Concurrent Jurisdiction

- Diversity Jurisdiction: the federal court has the authority to hear the case because the parties are diverse; meaning that the opposing parties come from different states.
- Requirements: (1) the parties must be citizens of different states AND (2) the dollar amount of the controversy must exceed $75,000.00.
  - Citizenship for a corporation: _____.

Subject Matter Jurisdiction: Concurrent Jurisdiction

- For example, a State of Florida plaintiff is claiming that a State of New York defendant owes him $40,000 for breaching a contract. In this instance, a federal court will dismiss the case for lack of subject matter jurisdiction or remand the case back to state court if one of the parties removed the case to federal court.

Personal Jurisdiction

- In addition to subject matter jurisdiction for each case, a court needs personal jurisdiction over the parties themselves.

Personal Jurisdiction

- Personal Jurisdiction is the judicial power over the parties in a case.
  - The power of a court to require a party (usually the defendant) or a witness to come before the court.
  - A plaintiff, by filing a lawsuit, gives the court personal jurisdiction over the plaintiff. The court must also have personal jurisdiction over the defendant.
- When will a state have jurisdiction over a defendant?

Personal Jurisdiction

- Non-Resident Defendant: Courts use a two-prong test to determine whether it has personal jurisdiction over a party who does not live in the same state where the court is located.
  - First, the court's jurisdiction must be authorized by a state long-arm statute that grants the court the ability to reach out and pull the non-resident defendant into its court. Typically, these statutes provide for jurisdiction of the non-resident defendant if (1) _____, (2) _____, or (3) _____.
  - The second prong requires fairness and due process. For each case, the constitutional question is whether the defendant has had enough "minimum contacts" within the state to require him/her to defend the lawsuit in that state.

Personal Jurisdiction

- Legal Implications in Cyberspace: Minimum Contacts over the Internet
  - In 1997, a federal district court in Pennsylvania issued a test for a minimum contacts analysis of personal jurisdiction based on one party's use of the Internet in its business. This became known as the **Zippo standard** (*Zippo Manufacturing Company v. Zippo Dot Com, Inc.*). The court adopted a sliding scale approach for measuring the number of minimum contacts based on the interactivity of a Web site owner via the user. The court explained the sliding scale by using an illustration of three points along the scale:
    - Passive
    - Interactive
    - Integral to the Business Model

Personal Jurisdiction

- Jurisdiction In Rem: courts also have personal jurisdiction over disputed property located within the state.
  - An action against the "things."
  - For example, the courts in Florida may determine rights to an orange grove in Florida, but not the ownership of a winery in California.

Standing

- Standing to Sue: the plaintiff must have some stake in the outcome of the lawsuit.

Venue

- The place where the case will be tried.
  - Generally, the lawsuit should be brought in the court where the parties work or reside, where the disputed interest in land is located, or where the occurrence causing the lawsuit took place.

State Court System

- Trial Courts
  - Limited Jurisdiction Trial Courts: hear cases of a specialized or limited matter.

State Court System

- Trial Courts
  - General Jurisdiction Trial Courts: hear cases of a general nature that are not within the jurisdiction of the limited jurisdiction trial courts.

State Court System

- Appellate Courts
  - An unsuccessful party in the trial court may appeal for relief.
  - Appellate courts typically limit their review to questions of law, rather than questions of fact.

State Court System

- State Supreme Court
  - The highest court in the state court system.
  - Decisions of the state supreme court are final, unless a question of law is involved that may be appealed to the United States Supreme Court.

Florida Court System

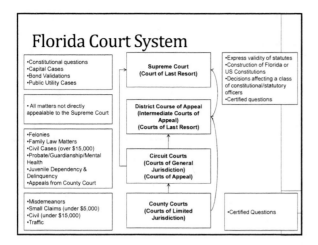

•Constitutional questions •Capital Cases •Bond Validations •Public Utility Cases	**Supreme Court** **(Court of Last Resort)**	•Express validity of statutes •Construction of Florida or US Constitutions •Decisions affecting a class of constitutional/statutory officers •Certified questions
• All matters not directly appealable to the Supreme Court	**District Course of Appeal** **(Intermediate Courts of Appeal)** **(Courts of Last Resort)**	
•Felonies •Family Law Matters •Civil Cases (over $15,000) •Probate/Guardianship/Mental Health •Juvenile Dependency & Delinquency •Appeals from County Court	**Circuit Courts** **(Courts of General Jurisdiction)** **(Courts of Appeal)**	
•Misdemeanors •Small Claims (under $5,000) •Civil (under $15,000) •Traffic	**County Courts** **(Courts of Limited Jurisdiction)**	•Certified Questions

Federal Court System

- Special Federal Courts
  - Bankruptcy
  - U.S. Tax Courts
  - U.S. Claims Courts
  - U.S. Court of International Trade

Federal Court System

- United States District Courts
  - Lawsuits in the federal system usually begin in the federal district courts.
  - These courts determine both the facts and law.

Federal Court System

- United States Courts of Appeal
  - If a party wishes to appeal the district court's decision, then the party brings the case before the appeals court, the circuit court, for that district.

Federal Court System

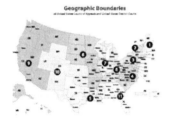

Federal Court System

- United States Supreme Court
  - Highest court in the land.
  - Appeals from circuit court decisions (or from the highest court of a state) may be heard by the United States Supreme Court.

Alternative Dispute Resolution

- The vast majority of disputes are settled out of court. Most do not even reach the point where a lawsuit is actually filed. If a complaint is filed, settlement usually occurs before the trial.
- The two most often used out-of-court methods of dispute resolution are mediation and arbitration.

Alternative Dispute Resolution

- Mediation: a third party (the mediator) helps the disputing parties to settle the case.

Alternative Dispute Resolution

- Arbitration: an out-of-court procedure in which a dispute is presented to one or more persons (arbitrators), whose decision is binding on the parties.

Chapter 3
Court Procedures

Chapter 3

Court Procedures

Civil Litigation

- Civil litigation is a term used to describe a dispute resolution process where parties and their attorney's argue their view of a civil controversy in a court of law.
  - Civil litigation includes contract disputes, lawsuits related to employment, negligence, bankruptcy, and property disputes.

Pre-Suit Considerations

- Factors for the parties to consider in determining whether to bring a lawsuit, defend a lawsuit, or settle a lawsuit:
  - probability of wining or losing;
  - loss of time by management and other personnel;
  - long-term effects on the relationship and reputation of the parties;
  - unpredictability of the legal system and possibility of error; and
  - legal fees.

Pre-Trial Litigation Process: Pleadings

- Pleadings: the paperwork that is filed with the court to begin and respond to a lawsuit.
  - The major pleadings are the complaint, the answer, the cross-complaint, and the reply.

Pre-Trial Litigation Process: Pleadings

- Plaintiff's Complaint: to begin a lawsuit, the plaintiff must file a complaint with the proper court.
  - Once a complaint has been filed with the court, the court issues a summons.

Pre-Trial Litigation Process: Pleadings

- Defendant's Answer: the defendant must file an answer to the plaintiff's complaint.
  - The defendant denies, affirms, or claims no knowledge of the accuracy of the plaintiff's allegations.
  - The defendant's answer is filed with the court and served on the plaintiff.
  - Consequences if the defendant does not file an answer?

Pre-Trial Litigation Process: Pleadings

- Counterclaim: a defendant who believes that the plaintiff has caused the defendant damages arising out of the very same set of facts as set forth in the complaint, can file a counterclaim.
- Cross-Claim: a defendant can also file a cross-claim when the defendant believes that a third party is either partially or fully liable for the damages that the plaintiff suffered.

Pre-Trial Litigation Process: Motions

- Motion to Transfer/Change Venue: a motion seeking to move the lawsuit to a more convenient location.

- Motion to Dismiss: a motion seeking to terminate the lawsuit due to plaintiff's failure to comply with proper procedure or failure to state a claim.

Pre-Trial Litigation Process: Motions

- Motion for Judgment on the Pleadings: this motion alleges that if all of the facts presented in the pleadings are true, the party making the motion would win the lawsuit when the law is applied to those facts.

Pre-Trial Litigation Process: Motions

- Motion for Summary Judgment: the trier of fact (i.e., the jury or, if there is no jury, the judge) determines the factual issues.
  - This motion asserts that there are no factual disputes to be decided by the jury and that the judge should apply the relevant law to the undisputed facts to decide the case.

Pre-Trial Litigation Process: Discovery

- During discovery, both parties engage in various activities to discover facts of the case from the other party and witnesses prior to trial.

Pre-Trial Litigation Process: Discovery

- The major forms of discovery are:
  - Depositions: sworn, oral testimony given by a party or witness prior to trial.
  - Interrogatories: written questions submitted by one party of a lawsuit to the other party.

Pre-Trial Litigation Process: Discovery

- Forms of discovery continued:
  - Requests for Admission: questions to the responding party phrased in an "admit" or "deny" format, giving no opportunity for explanation, and binding the responding party to its admissions.

  - Requests for Production: one party to a lawsuit may request that the other party produce documents, videos, photographs that are relevant to the case prior to trial.

  - Requests for Examination: in cases that concern the physical or mental condition of a party, a court can order the party to submit to certain physical or mental examinations to determine the extent of the alleged injuries.

_____

_____

_____

_____

_____

_____

_____

Pre-Trial Litigation: Settlement Conference

- Federal court rules and state court rules permit the court to direct the attorney's or parties to appear before the court for a pretrial hearing or settlement conference.

_____

_____

_____

_____

_____

_____

_____

Stages of a Trial

- Jury Selection: the pool of potential jurors is usually selected from voter or automobile registration lists.
  - The trial judge or the attorneys for the parties ask a panel of prospective jurors to answer a series of questions (a.k.a. *voir dire*).
  - Florida: _____ jurors for a civil case and _____ jurors for a criminal case, except _____.

_____

_____

_____

_____

_____

_____

_____

Stages of a Trial

- Opening Statements: each party's attorney is allowed to make an opening statement to the jury.
- Examination of Witnesses:
  - Direct Examination: after the witness is sworn in, the plaintiff's attorney questions the witness.
  - Cross-Examination: after the plaintiff's attorney has completed his or her questions, the defendant's attorney can question the witness.
  - Re-Direct: after cross-examination, the attorney who called the witness has a final opportunity to ask questions.

Stages of a Trial

- Defendant's Case: the defendant's case proceeds after the plaintiff has concluded his or her case.
- Rebuttal: after the defendant's attorney has completed calling witnesses, the plaintiff's attorney has a rebuttal.
- Closing Argument: after both sides have presented all of their evidence, counsel for each party makes a closing argument.

Stages of a Trial

- Jury Instructions: at the end of closing arguments, the judge reads jury instructions to the jury.
- Jury Deliberation: the jury then retires to the jury room to deliberate its findings.
  - If the jury cannot agree on a verdict, this is known as a hung jury and the litigants must start the process all over again with a new jury.

Stages of a Trial

- Verdict: the jury then renders a verdict setting forth its findings and the amount of damages, if any.
  - Standards of Proof:
    - Civil:_____.
    - Criminal:_____.

Post Litigation

- Dispositive Motions: motions asking the trial court to dispose of a party's claims for affirmative relief, to alter or disregard the jury's verdict, or to order a new trial.

Post-Litigation

- Motion for Directed Verdict: a motion for the judge to take the decision out of the jury's hands and direct a verdict for the moving party because the non-moving party has failed to provide sufficient evidence to prevail on its claims.

Post-Litigation

- Motion for Judgment Notwithstanding the Verdict (Motion for J.N.O.V.): a motion asking the court to enter judgment in favor of the moving party, despite the jury's verdict in favor of the non-moving party.

Post-Litigation

- Motion for New Trial: a motion asserting that the trial was so fundamentally flawed that a new trial is required to prevent a miscarriage of justice.

Appellate Procedure

- What is filed with the appellate court? Generally:
  - a notice of appeal;
  - a record or transcript of the pleadings, motions, hearings, and trial before the trial court; and
  - briefs.

Appellate Procedure

- Based on the arguments raised in the briefs and, if there is one, at oral argument, the appellate court may:
  - affirm;
  - reverse and remand; or
  - reverse and render a new judgment or ruling.

Chapter 6
Intentional Torts & Negligence

Chapter 6

Intentional Torts

Torts

- Tort is the French word for a "wrong."
  - Tort law protects a variety of injuries and provides remedies for the injuries.
  - A tort is a violation of a duty imposed by civil law.

Tort Law v. Criminal Law

Type of Obligation	Tort Law	Criminal Law
Creation of Obligation	Civil law imposes duties of conduct.	Criminal law prohibits certain conduct.
Enforcement of Obligation	Lawsuit by plaintiff.	Prosecution by the government.
Possible Result	Money damages for plaintiff.	Punishment for defendant (prison and/or fine).

Torts

- Damages
  - Compensatory Damages: money intended to restore the plaintiff to the position she/he was in prior to the injury.

  - Punitive Damages: money intended to punish the tortfeasor (the defendant) for conduct that is extreme and outrageous.

_____

_____

_____

_____

_____

_____

Intentional Torts

- Harm caused by a deliberate action.
  - Even if the harm is unintended, the defendant still may be liable for an intentional tort.
    - Example: intentionally throwing a snowball at a friend is a deliberate act; if the snowball permanently damages his eye, the defendant is probably liable for the intentional tort of battery.

_____

_____

_____

_____

_____

_____

Intentional Torts Against Persons

- Assault
  - Assault is the fear of immediate harm or offensive contact or any action that stimulates reasonable apprehension of imminent harm.

_____

_____

_____

_____

_____

_____

_____

Intentional Torts Against Persons

- Battery
  - Battery is unauthorized and harmful or offensive physical contact with another person.

Intentional Torts Against Persons

- False Imprisonment
  - False imprisonment is the intentional confinement or restraint of another person without authority or justification and without that person's consent.
    - Shopkeeper's Privilege

Intentional Torts Against Persons

- Intentional Infliction of Emotional Distress (IIED)
  - Intentional infliction of emotional distress is the disturbance of a person's peace of mind by another's outrageous conduct.

Intentional Torts Against Persons

- Invasion of Privacy
  - In tort law, the invasion of privacy refers to four distinct torts:
    - Appropriation.
    - Intrusion upon a person's private life.
    - Placing someone in a false light.
    - Public disclosure of private facts.

Intentional Torts Against Property

- Trespass to Real Property
  - Unauthorized entry onto the plaintiff's land, either by a person or by an object the person caused to enter the land.
- Trespass to Personal Property
  - Unjustified interference with another person's personal property or interference with that person's enjoyment of his or her personal property.

Intentional Torts Against Property

- Conversion
  - The civil counterpart to theft.
  - Intended to reimburse a party who suffered damages as a result of theft or other substantial interference with a party's ownership.
  - Fairness requires that the tortfeasor reimburse the injured party for the full value of the property.
    - Example: the controller of a corporation embezzles corporate funds and covers up the discrepancies on financial statements.

Other Intentional Torts

- Defamation
  - A false communication of fact by the defendant to a third person that harms the plaintiff's reputation.
  - The statement must be false, not merely unkind. And, a statement of pure opinion is not actionable.
    - Slander is oral.
    - Libel involves writing, broadcasting, or any other recorded medium.
  - Publication requirement.
  - Public figure test: if the victim is a public figure, the defamation must have been committed with
    _____.

Other Intentional Torts

- Fraud
  - Fraud is a false, material representation of fact that the defendant either knows to be false or recklessly makes knowing that the information is incomplete.

Defenses to Intentional Torts

- Consent
  - Consent is the actual or apparent willingness for conduct of another to occur.
  - Consent must be informed and freely given.

Defenses to Intentional Torts

- Self-Defense
  - An individual defending his or her life or physical well-being, either from real or apparent danger, may use reasonably necessary force, or resort to reasonably necessary action, to prevent harmful contact.
- Defense or Assistance of Others
  - An individual can act in a reasonable manner to protect or assist others who are in real or apparent danger.
- Defense of Property
  - An individual may use reasonable force to remove an intruder from the individual's home or to restrain the intruder for a reasonable time.

Defenses to Defamation

- Privilege
  - The two types of privilege are absolute privilege and qualified privilege.
    - Absolute privilege exists in courtrooms and legislative hearings.
    - Qualified privilege exists between two people who have a legitimate need to exchange information.

Negligence

- Negligence is defined as the omission to do something which a reasonable person would do or something which a prudent and reasonable person would not do.

Negligence

- To be successful in a negligence lawsuit, the plaintiff must prove the elements of negligence, which are:
  - defendant owed a duty of care to the plaintiff;
  - defendant breached that duty of care;
  - plaintiff suffered an injury; and
  - the defendant's negligent act caused the plaintiff's injury.

_____

_____

_____

_____

_____

_____

Negligence

- Duty
  - A person has a legal duty to act reasonably and avoid harming others.
    - This general duty imposed on every party is to act like a reasonably prudent person would under the circumstances.
  - Duty of Professionals.

_____

_____

_____

_____

_____

_____

_____

Negligence

VISITOR'S STATUS	DESCRIPTION	DUTIES OF LANDOWNER
Public Invitee	"A person who is invited to enter or remain on land as a member of the public for a purpose for which the land is held open to the public."	To _____ or _____ of dangers that the owner knows or _____, by the use of _____, and which the visitor cannot or should not know of by the use of _____
Business Invitee	"A person who is invited to enter or remain on land for a purpose directly or indirectly connected with business dealings with the possessor of the land."	
Licensee by Invitation	A social guest.	
Uninvited Licensee	"Persons who chose to come upon the premises solely for their own convenience without invitation either expressed or reasonably implied under the circumstances."	To refrain from _____ or _____ injury.
Trespasser	Someone "who enters the premises of another without license, invitation, or other right, and intrudes for some definite purpose of his own, or at his own convenience, or merely as an idler with no apparent purpose, other than perhaps to satisfy his curiosity."	

_____

_____

_____

_____

_____

_____

_____

Negligence

- Breach of Duty
  - Once the court finds that the defendant actually owed the plaintiff a duty of care, it must determine whether the defendant breached this duty.
  - A breach of the duty of care is the failure to exercise care.

Negligence

- Causation

  - Actual cause. This is the "but for" test. The question that must be answered is *but for (except for) the breach of duty by the tortfeasor, would the injured party have suffered damages*?

  - Proximate cause. Once actual cause is proved, the plaintiff must prove that the plaintiff's injuries were foreseeable.

Negligence

- Damages

  - Plaintiff must prove legal injury.

Special Negligence Doctrines

- *Res Ipsa Loquitur*
  - The facts imply that the defendant's negligence was the cause of the accident.

Special Negligence Doctrines

- Good Samaritan Statutes
  - Relieves medical professionals from liability for injury caused by their ordinary negligence when they stop and render aid to victims in emergency situations such as automobile accidents.

Special Negligence Doctrines

- Dram Shop Liability
  - Many states make a tavern and bartender liable for injuries caused to or by patrons who are served too much alcohol.

Negligence

- Defenses
  - Assumption of Risk.

  - Contributory Negligence.

  - Comparative Negligence.

Negligence

- Assumption of Risk
  - Requires the defendant to show that the plaintiff knew the risk was present, understood its nature, and voluntarily chose to incur the risk.

Negligence

- Contributory Negligence
  - Under the common law doctrine of contributory negligence, a plaintiff who is partially at fault for his or her own injury cannot recover against the negligent defendant.

Negligence

- Comparative Negligence
  - Under this doctrine, damages are apportioned according to fault.

Chapter 10
Criminal Law

Chapter 10

Criminal Law

Definition of Crime

- A crime is any act done by an individual in violation of the duties he or she owes to society and for the breach of which the law provides that the wrongdoer shall make amends to the public.

Classifications of Crime

- Felonies.
  - Most serious kinds of crimes.
  - Felonies are often subdivided by type of punishment:
    - capital felonies;
    - life felonies;
    - first degree felonies;
    - second degree felonies; and
    - third degree felonies.

Classification of Crimes

- Misdemeanors.
  - Less serious then felonies.
  - First degree misdemeanor;
  - Second degree misdemeanor.

- Violations/Petty offenses.
  - Crimes such as jaywalking and traffic violations.

_____

_____

_____

_____

_____

_____

_____

Common Elements of Crime

- An analysis of criminal liability involves three questions:
- (1) Did the defendant actually commit the prohibited act?
- (2) Did the defendant have a culpable state of mind?
- (3) Does the law give the defendant a defense (such as self-defense)?

_____

_____

_____

_____

_____

_____

_____

Criminal Act

- The defendant must have actually performed the prohibited act.
  - Example: no criminal act: Dan Deviant thinks about assaulting Veronica Victim, but does nothing about it. No crime.
- Sometimes, an act of omission can also sometimes be crime.

_____

_____

_____

_____

_____

_____

_____

Criminal Intent

- It is often said that "the act will not make a person guilty unless the mind is also guilty."
  - Example: no criminal intent: Ivan Innocent, through no intent, negligence, or other fault of his own, collides with Veronica Victim and kills her. No crime.
- The words and phrases contained in criminal statutes to express the guilty mind include: *intentionally*, *knowingly*, *maliciously*, and *willfully*.
  - Example: Arson:

    Any person who *willfully* and *unlawfully*, or while in the commission of any felony, by fire or explosion, damages or causes to be damaged:

    (a) Any dwelling, whether occupied or not, or its contents;

    (b) Any structure…;

    is guilty of arson in the first degree, which constitutes a felony of the first degree, punishable as provided…

Violent Crimes

- Robbery
  - At common law, robbery is defined as the taking of personal property from another person by the use of fear or force.
  - Florida: "Robbery" means the taking of money or other property which may be the subject of larceny from the person or custody of another, with intent to either permanently or temporarily deprive the person or the owner of the money or other property, when in the course of the taking there is the use of force, violence, assault, or putting in fear.
- Other violent crimes: murder, assault, battery.

Property Crimes

- Burglary
  - At common law, burglary was the breaking and entering the dwelling house of another at night with the intent to commit a felony.
- Larceny
  - At common law, larceny is the taking of personal property with the intent to steal it.

Property Crimes

- Arson
  - At common law, arson was defined as the malicious or willful burning of the dwelling of another person.
- Forgery
  - Fraudulently making or altering a written document that affects the legal liability of another person.

White Collar Crimes

- Embezzlement
  - Fraudulent conversion of property or money owned by one person but entrusted to another.
- Mail and Wire Fraud
  - Use of mail, telephone, radio, or television to further or execute a scheme to defraud. These federal criminal statutes are used against a wide range of crimes, including kickbacks to private employees and bribery of public officials.

White Collar Crimes

- Bribery
  - Illegal payments or offers to pay to a political campaign, to governmental officials, or to other persons such as the employees of a competing firm, for the purpose of receiving favorable treatment, for proprietary information, or other assistance.
    - Bribery is covered in both federal and state statutes.
- Bankruptcy Fraud
  - Filing false claims by creditors or debtors, fraudulent transfer or concealment of assets, or obtaining credit with the specific intent to avoid paying debts.

White Collar Crimes

- Insider Trading
  - Federal securities statutes that prohibit corporate insiders who have access to certain information that is not available to the public from trading their company's stock based on the insider knowledge.
    - Insiders can be executives, managers, corporate counsel, consultants, brokers.

Corporate Criminal Liability

- A corporation may be criminally liable if:
  - an agent or employee of the corporation (a) commits a criminal act within the scope of employment and (b) the criminal act violates a statute whose purpose it is to impose liability on the corporation; or
  - it failed to perform a specific affirmative duty required by law; or
  - the crime was authorized, requested, commanded, committed, or recklessly tolerated by a "high managerial agent."

Corporate Criminal Liability

- A corporate officer or director may be personally liable for:
  - his/her own criminal acts, whether for personal benefit or on behalf of the corporation; and
  - under certain circumstances for crimes committed by his or her subordinates.
- In 2002, the Sarbanes-Oxley Act imposed criminal liability for officers, directors, and majority shareholders of corporations that falsify financial disclosures and provides up to 20 years of incarceration for an employee that destroys documents relevant to a government agency investigation.

General Defenses to Crimes

- Infancy
  - Bars criminal liability for children who are under a certain age and/or do not understand a particular act is wrong.
- Involuntary Intoxication
  - A person, by force, by mistake, or by some situation beyond his/her control, ingests or has injected an intoxicating substance.

General Defenses to Crimes

- Insanity
  - A defense if the alleged crime occurred while the defendant lacked the mental capacity for the required criminal intent.
  - Three tests:
    - Model Penal Code test.
    - M' Naghten test.
    - Irresistible impulse test.

General Defenses to Crimes

- Mistake
  - Mistake of Fact depends on whether it negates the required mental state.
    - If Nora walks off with Tammie's child (who resembles Nora's child) and Nora returns the child as soon as she discovers her mistake, Nora is not guilty of kidnapping.
  - Mistake of Law is a defense when the person honestly did not know that he/she was breaking the law and: (1) the law was not published or otherwise made known to the public or (2) the person relied on a wrong but official statement of the law, such as a statute, court order, or administrative order.

General Defenses to Crimes

- Self-Defense
  - Generally, people can use the amount of force that is reasonably necessary to protect themselves, their houses or other property, or to prevent a crime.
- Entrapment
  - A criminal defense if the criminal act was induced by the government, with criminal intent originating from the police. If the accused was predisposed to commit the crime, then entrapment is not a defense.
- Statute of Limitations
  - Statutorily defined periods of time within which a legal action must be brought.

General Defenses to Crimes

- Immunity
  - Immunity from prosecution is sometimes extended to actual or potential criminal defendants, usually to induce testimony and information from them.

Constitutional Rights for an Accused

- The Fourth Amendment's protection from unreasonable searches and seizures and require that a search or arrest warrant shall be based on probable cause.
  - Searches without a warrant are permitted in some situations.
- The Fifth Amendment's prohibition against double jeopardy and prohibition against self-incrimination.
- The Sixth Amendment's guarantees of the rights to a criminal defendant to a speedy trial, trial by jury, public trial, and the right to confront witnesses and to counsel.
- The Eighth Amendment's prohibition against excessive bail and fines and cruel and unusual punishment.
  - For example, the Eighth Amendment prohibits the torture of criminals.

Constitutional Rights of an Accused

- The Exclusionary Rule: any evidence obtained in violation of the accused's Fourth, Fifth, or Sixth Amendment rights, as well as any evidence derived from the illegally obtained evidence, is not admissible.

_____

_____

_____

_____

_____

_____

Constitutional Rights of an Accused

- The Miranda Rule: individuals who are arrested must be informed that they have a right to remain silent and a right to an attorney. These rights may be waived if the waiver is knowing and voluntary.

_____

_____

_____

_____

_____

_____

Chapter 11
Nature and Terminology

Chapter 11

Nature and Terminology

What is a Contract?

- A widely recognized definition of a contract is provided by the Restatement (Second) of Contracts: "A contract is a promise or a set of promises for the breach of which the law gives a remedy or the performance of which the law in some way recognizes a duty."
  - A promise or a set of promises enforceable by law.

The Parties to a Contract

- Every contract involves at least two parties, the offeror and offeree.
  - The offeror is the person who makes an offer to enter into a contract.
  - The offeree is the party to whom the offer is made.

Elements of a Contract

- To be an enforceable contract, there are four requirements that must be met:
  1. Agreement
  2. Consideration
  3. Contractual Capacity
  4. Legality

Sources of Contract Law

- Common Law.
  - Contracts relating to real estate, employment, and insurance are types of contracts generally governed by common law.
- Uniform Commercial Code.
  - These are the contracts for sale and lease of goods under Article 2 and 2A.
    - A contract for the lease of a copying machine is governed by the UCC.
- Restatement (Second) of Contracts.
  - Attempted to codify what its members regarded as the best rulings of contract law.

Classifications of Contracts: Bilateral and Unilateral

- Bilateral Contract: a promise for a promise. Two promises and two performances.
  - For example, a baseball team owner says to Barry Base, "I'll pay you $2 million to play first base for the St. Pete Sunrays next season." Barry says, "It's a deal."
    - The owner is now bound to pay Barry $2 million and Barry is obligated to show up at spring training and play for the Sunrays.

Classifications of Contracts: Bilateral and Unilateral

- Unilateral Contract: a promise for an act.
  - For example, Gregg offers Glenn $15 to mow Gregg's yard.
- When the offeree begins performance of a unilateral contract and the offeror attempts to revoke the offer, most courts and the Restatement (Second) of Contracts states:

  _____.

Classifications of Contracts: Express and Implied

- Express Contract: a contract that is expressed in written or oral words.
  - The contract between the team owner and Barry is an express contract because the parties explicitly stated what Barry will do, where and when he will play baseball, and how much he will be paid.

Classifications of Contracts: Express and Implied

- Implied-in-Fact Contract: implied from the conduct of the parties. The following elements must be established to create an implied-in-fact contract:
  1. the plaintiff provided property or services to the defendant,
  2. the plaintiff expected to be paid for the property or services (i.e., the property or services were not a gift), and
  3. the defendant was given the opportunity to reject the service or property and failed to do so.

Classifications of Contracts: Express and Implied Continued

- Implied-in-Law Contract (Quasi Contract): a fictional contract where the court awards damages to a plaintiff for providing work or services to a defendant.
  - Recovery generally is based on the reasonable value of the services received by the defendant.

Classifications of Contracts: Formal and Informal

- Formal Contract: a contract that requires a special form or method of creation. The Restatement (Second) of Contracts identifies the following types of formal contracts:
  - Contract Under Seal.
  - Negotiable Instruments.
  - Letter of Credit.

Classifications of Contracts: Formal and Informal Continued

- Informal Contract (or Simple Contract): a contract that does not require a specified form or method of formation in order to be valid.
  - The vast majority of contracts are informal. Examples: leases, sales contracts, and service contracts.

Classification by Enforcability

- Valid Contract: a contract that meets all of the essential elements to establish a contract.

- Void Contract: a contract that has no legal effect.

- Voidable Contract: a contract where at least one party has the option to avoid his or her contractual obligations.

- Unenforceable Contract: a contract where there is a legal defense to the enforcement of the contract.

Executed and Executory Contracts

- Executory Contract: a contract that has not been performed by one or more parties.
  - Recall Barry Base, who agreed to play baseball for the St. Pete Sunrays. The moment Barry and the team owner strike their bargain, they have an executory, bilateral, express contract.
- Executed Contract: a completed contract.

Chapter 12
Agreement

Chapter 12

Agreement

Mutual Assent

- The manner in which parties usually show mutual assent is by offer and acceptance.

Offer

- Offer: The Restatement (Second) of Contracts defines an offer as: "The manifestation of willingness to enter into a bargain, so made as to justify another person in understanding that his/her assent to that bargain is invited and will conclude it."

Offer

- Under common law, for an offer to be effective, the following three elements are required:
  1. the offeror must objectively intend to be bound by the offer;
  2. the terms of the offer must be definite or reasonably certain; and
  3. the offer must be communicated to the offeree.

Offer: Intention

- The intent to enter a contract is determined using the objective theory of contracts.
  - That is, whether a reasonable person viewing the circumstances would conclude that the parties intended to be legally bound.
- When an agreement is a business transaction, there is a strong presumption that the parties intended the agreement to be legally enforceable.
  - *Lucy v. Zehmer*

Offer: Intention

- Problems With Intent
  - Offers made in anger or jest.

  - Opinions.

  - Preliminary negotiations.

Offer: Definite Terms

- To be considered definite, an offer generally must contain the following terms:
  - identification of the parties;
  - the identity of subject matter and quantity;
  - the consideration to be paid; and
  - the time of performance.
- However, missing terms may be supplied by courts. The trend of the UCC and modern case law is to supply reasonable terms – even material ones.

Offer: Communication

- An offer cannot be accepted if it is not communicated to the offeree by the offeror.
  - For example, suppose Mr. Smith, the CEO of Rocky Bull Apparel, Inc., wants to sell its retail store to Bull Haven Corporation. Mr. Smith puts the offer in writing, but he does not send it. Mr. Baker, the CEO of Bull Haven Corporation, visits Mr. Smith and sees the written offer lying on Mr. Smith's desk. There is no offer to be accepted, though, because Mr. Smith never communicated the offer to the CEO of Bull Haven Corporation.

Revoking an Offer

- By the offeror: communicating the withdrawal of the offer to the offeree prior to the offeree's acceptance.
  - Exceptions to this easy right to withdraw:
    - Option contracts;
    - Promissory estoppel; and
    - Unilateral contracts.

Rejecting an Offer

- By the Offeree: an offer is terminated if the offeree rejects it.
  - Generally, a rejection is not effective until it is actually received by the offeror.
  - Any subsequent attempt by the offeree to "accept" is ineffective and will be a new offer, which the original offeror (now the offeree) may accept.

Counteroffer

- By the offeree: a response by an offeree that contains terms and conditions different from or in addition to those of the offer.
  - A counteroffer operates a rejection.

Offers Terminated as a Matter of Law

- Destruction of subject matter.

- Lapse of time.

- Death or incompetence.

- Illegality.

4

Special Offer Scenarios

- Advertisements: generally treated as invitations to make an offer.
  - An advertisement will be an offer if it is so specific that it is evident that the advertiser has the intent to bind itself to the terms of the advertisement.

Acceptance

- A voluntary act by the offeree – either in the form of words or of conduct – which indicates agreement to the terms of the offer.
- The "Mirror Image" Rule requires the offeree to accept the offeror's terms exactly. If the offeree's acceptance materially changes, adds to, or deletes any terms in the original offer, the offeree's attempted acceptance is deemed to constitute a counteroffer, not an acceptance.

Acceptance

- The UCC modifies the "Mirror Image Rule" for the sale of goods.
- Under the UCC, an acceptance that adds additional or different terms will often create a contract.

Acceptance by Silence

- Generally, silence cannot constitute acceptance.
- Exceptions:
  - Acts consistent with acceptance.

  - Prior dealings.

  - Unilateral contracts.

Chapter 13
Consideration

Chapter 13

Consideration

Consideration

- PROMISE ONE. In a delirious burst of affection, I, Professor Stowell, say to you, my class of wonderful students, "You've been such a great class all semester. Next week, I'm going to give you each a check for $50." That evening, I have second thoughts and decide that I might like the class next semester better. The following week, in class, I announce I have changed my mind. A student sues for his $50.00. Should a court enforce my promise?

Consideration

- PROMISE TWO. After class, I promise a student a part-time job as a research assistant for the rest of the semester. "You can start on Monday," I tell the student "and we'll work out pay, the hours, and all the details then." "You mean I can give up my job at Five-Star Pizza?" asks the ecstatic student. "Sure thing," I say. On Monday, I inform the student that I lost funding for the position due to budget cuts in the State of Florida. The student is unable to get her job back at Five-Star Pizza and sues me.

Consideration

- PROMISE THREE. I announce in class that I will be selling my iPad at the end of the semester for $75. After class, a student says she'd like to buy the iPad, but can only afford to pay $50. I frown and say, "It is worth more than that." But, the student looks so heartbroken that I say, "Okay, you may have the iPad on May 15th." On that date, the student shows up with the $50. I explain that another student offered me the full $75 for the iPad, so I sold it. The student buys a iPad for $100 and sues me.

Consideration

- PROMISE FOUR. I make no promise at all. In fact, I announce in class that I will be unable to attend the next class because some of the Food Network stars will be in town and I want to meet them. The students are crushed at the idea of missing a Business Law class. One student says, "Don't do this to us, Professor! I'll pay you twenty bucks if you'll be here to teach us." Other students chime in, and through the tears and emotion, the students promise a total of $1,000 if I'll do my job. I agree. When I arrive to teach the next class, the students refuse to pay, and I sue.

Consideration

- The doctrine of consideration ensures that promises are enforced only where the parties have exchanged something of value in the eye of the law.
- Consideration consists of two elements: (1) something of legal value must be given and (2) there must be a bargained-for exchange.

Legal Value

- Legally sufficient (legal value) consideration may take the form of:
  - a promise that the promisee is not otherwise obligated to undertake;
  - tangible payment;
  - performing an action that the promisee is not otherwise obligated to undertake; or
  - forebearance of a legal right that the promisee is otherwise entitled to exercise.

Bargained-For Exchange

- Consideration is bargained-for if it is sought by the promisor in exchange for the promisor's promise and given by the promisee in exchange for the promisor's promise.
  - This is primarily to distinguish contracts from gifts.

How Much Consideration?

- Generally, courts will not inquire into the sufficiency of the consideration.
  - If there is fraud, duress, undue influence, or incompetence, a court may look at the adequacy of the consideration.

Inadequate Consideration

- Gift promises.

- Pre-existing duty rule.
  - Exception: modification.

  - Exception: additional work.

  - Exception: unforeseen circumstances.

Inadequate Consideration

- Past consideration.

- Moral obligations.

- Illegal consideration.

- Illusory contracts.

- Options to cancel at any time.

Promises Enforceable Without Consideration

- The following elements must be shown for the doctrine of promissory estoppel to apply:
  - the promisor made a promise;
  - the promisor should have reasonably expected the promisee to rely on the promise;
  - the promisee relied on the promise; and
  - injustice would be caused if the promise was not enforced.

Consideration

- Promise One Result:_____
  _____
- Promise Two Result: _____
  _____
- Promise Three Result: _____
  _____
- Promise Four Result: _____
  _____

Chapter 14
Capacity

Chapter 14

Capacity and Legality

Contractual Capacity

- Definition: the legal ability to enter into a contract.
- Problems with capacity make a contract voidable meaning one party has the option either to enforce or terminate the agreement.

Contractual Capacity

- Certain persons are generally not considered to have sufficient capacity to be bound by their contracts:
  - Minors;
  - Intoxicated persons; and
  - Mentally incapacitated persons.

Contractual Capacity - Minority

- Minors: today, in almost all states, unmarried persons under the age of eighteen (18) are considered minors.

Contractual Capacity - Minority

- Disaffirmance: to protect minors, the law recognizes the infancy doctrine, which gives minors the right to disaffirm (cancel) most contracts they have entered into with adults.
  - Under the infancy doctrine, a minor has the option of choosing whether to enforce the contract.
  - Timing of Disaffirmance?

Contractual Capacity - Minority

- States differ on the extent of a minor's obligations when the minor disaffirms a contract.
  - Most states require the minor to return any consideration (goods) in the minor's possession or control.
  - A number of states are now holding that the minor has a duty of restitution.

Contractual Capacity - Minority

- Misrepresentations Regarding Age: under the common law, a minor who misrepresented his/her age would still have the right to disaffirm the contract.
  - Now,
    - Some states still allow for the minor to disaffirm the contract entirely.
    - Some statutes prohibit disaffirmance.
    - Many states, though, prohibit disaffirmance of executed contracts unless the minor can return the consideration received.

Contractual Capacity - Minority

- Ratification: if a minor does not disaffirm a contract either during the period of minority or within a reasonable time after reaching the age of majority, the contract is considered ratified.

Contractual Capacity - Minority

- Necessaries of Life: when minors contract for the necessaries of life, they are obligated to pay for those necessaries of life.
  - Items such as food, clothing, shelter, and medical services are generally considered necessaries of life. Goods and services such as automobiles, tools of trade, education, and vocational training have also been found to be necessaries of life in some situations.
  - The minor is obligated to pay the reasonable value of the goods or services received.

Contractual Capacity - Minority

- Parental Liability: parents will be liable if a parent co-signs the contract and, thereby, assumes personal liability for performance of the contract.

Contractual Capacity - Intoxication

- Most states provide that contracts entered into by certain intoxicated persons are voidable by that person.
- The intoxication may occur because of alcohol or drugs.
- Under the majority rule, the contract is voidable only if the person was so intoxicated when the contract was entered into that he was incapable of understanding or comprehending the nature of the transaction.

Contractual Capacity - Intoxication

- Disaffirmance: a person can disaffirm the contract based on intoxication.
  - If the intoxicated person disaffirms the contract, the intoxicated person, generally, must be returned to the status quo. In turn, the intoxicated person, generally, must return the consideration received under the contract to the other party and make restitution that returns the other party to the status quo.

Contractual Capacity - Intoxication

- Ratification: after becoming sober, an intoxicated person can ratify the contracts he entered into while intoxicated.
- Intoxicated persons are liable to pay the reasonable value for necessaries of life they receive.

Contractual Capacity – Mental Incompetency

- The law protects people suffering from substantial mental incapacity from enforcement of contracts against them because such persons may not understand the consequences of their actions in entering into a contract.
- The law requires the person to be mentally incompetent at the time of entering into the contract.

Contractual Capacity – Mental Incompetency

- Void Contract: Person under Guardianship: In certain cases, a relative, loved one, or other interested party may institute a legal action to have someone declared legally incompetent. If the person is declared incompetent, the court will make that person a ward of the court and appoint a guardian to act on that person's behalf. Any contract entered into by a person who has been declared incompetent is void.

Contractual Capacity – Mental Incompetency

- Voidable Contract: A contract will be voidable by a person who is incompetent at the time the contract was formed, but not previously determined by the court to be mentally incompetent. Unless the other party does not have contractual capacity, he or she does not have the option to avoid the contract.

Contractual Capacity – Mental Incompetency

- A person who has dealt with a mentally incompetent person must place that person in status quo if the contract is either void or voided by the mentally incompetent person.
- Mentally incompetent persons must return any consideration and must pay the reasonable value for the necessaries of life they receive.

Legality: Illegal Agreements

- Usury: state usury laws are an upper limit on the annual interest rate that can be charged on certain types of loans. Lenders who charge a higher rate than the state limit are guilty of usury.
- Gambling: all states have legislation regarding gambling and the U.S. courts generally refuse to recognize the enforceability of a gambling agreement.

Legality: Licensing

- All states require members of certain professions and occupations to be licensed by the state in which they practice.
  - Problems arise if an unlicensed person tries to collect payment for services provided to another under a contract. Some statutes expressly provide that unlicensed persons cannot enforce contracts to provide these services. If the statute is silent, enforcement depends on whether it is a regulatory statute or a revenue-raising statute.

Legality: Licensing

- Regulatory Statutes: licensing statutes that are enacted to protect the public are called regulatory statutes.
  - Generally, unlicensed persons cannot recover payment for services that a regulatory statute requires a licensed person to provide.

Legality: Licensing

- Revenue-Raising Statutes: licensing statutes enacted to raise money for the government.
  - A person who provides services pursuant to a contract without the appropriate license required by such a statute can enforce the contract and recover payment for services rendered.

Legality: Covenants Not to Compete

- Restrictive Covenants in the Sale of a Business: many contracts for the sale of a business require the seller not to open a competing business within a defined area.
  - To be enforceable, the geographic restriction must be reasonable, and it must be effective only for a reasonable period of time after the sale is completed.

Legality: Covenants Not to Compete

- Restrictive Covenants in Employment Contracts: many employment contracts require the employee to refrain from working for a competitor or starting a new business in competition with the employer for a reasonable period of time, and within a reasonably defined geographic area, after the employment relationship ends.

Chapter 16
Statute of Frauds

Chapter 16

Statute of Frauds

Statute of Frauds

- In 1677, the British Parliament passed "An Act for the Prevention of Frauds and Perjuries," generally referred to as the Statute of Frauds.
  - This act was designed to prevent the perpetration of frauds arising out of purely oral agreements.
  - The act required that there be evidence in writing (called a memorandum) about certain kinds of contracts that the Parliament considered subject to perjury, abuses, and fraud.
- Today, almost all states have enacted a Statute of Frauds that requires certain types of contracts to be in writing.

Scope of the Statute of Frauds

- The Statute of Frauds relates to six kinds of contracts that require written evidence.
  - First, a contract for the sale of land or an interest therein.
    - This includes real estate contracts, leases, easements, and mortgages.
      - Exception: most states, by statute, allow for an oral lease for one year or less.

Scope of the Statute of Frauds

- Second, a contract not to be performed within one year.
  - If it is possible for a contract to be performed within a year, a memorandum is not necessary.

Scope of the Statute of Frauds

Agreements That Cannot Be Performed Within One Year

Type of Agreement	Enforceability
An offer of employment for three years.	Must be in writing to be enforceable (cannot be performed within one year).
"As long as you work here at Five Star Pizza, you may have Friday's off."	Enforceable whether it is oral or written since the employee might quit a week later.

Scope of the Statute of Frauds

- Third, a contract for the sale of goods for a price of $500.00 or more.
  - This requirement is found in the Uniform Commercial Code (UCC), section 2-201.

Scope of the Statute of Frauds

- Fourth, a promise by one person to pay the debt of another.
  - Relates to contracts of guaranty.

Scope of the Statute of Frauds

- Fifth, a promise made in consideration of marriage.
  - Intended to involve dowry – the agreement of a woman (or her father) to pay consideration to the intended husband.
  - Although dowry agreements are not common in the United States, prenuptial agreements are covered by the Statute of Frauds.

Scope of the Statute of Frauds

- Sixth, a promise by the personal representative of an estate to pay a debt of the estate out of his/her own funds.

Statute of Frauds Exceptions

- Full Performance: Sale or Transfer of Interest in Real Property: if the seller completely performs her side of a contract for the sale or transfer of interest in real property, a court is likely to enforce the agreement even if it is oral.

Statute of Frauds Exceptions

- Part Performance: Sale or Transfer of Interest in Real Property:
  - Paid part of the purchase price,
  - and either:
    - entered upon the land; or
    - made improvements to it.

Statute of Frauds Exceptions

- Part Performance: Sale of Goods over $500.00:
  - Under the UCC, an oral contract is enforceable to the extent that the seller has accepted payment or the buyer has accepted delivery of the goods covered by the oral contract.

Statute of Frauds Exceptions

- Promissory Estoppel: The Restatement (Second) of Contracts version of promissory estoppel provides that if the parties enter into an oral contract that should be in writing under the Statute of Frauds, the oral promise is enforceable against the promisor if these three conditions are met: (1) the promise induces action or forbearance of action by another, (2) the reliance on the oral promise was foreseeable, and (3) injustice can be avoided only by enforcing the oral promise.

The Memorandum of Writing

- The memorandum in writing must meet the following requirements:
  - It must identify all the essential terms of the parties' agreement.
  - It must have been signed by the party being charged (sued).

Chapter 48
Personal Property

Chapter 48

Personal Property

Property

- There are two kinds of property: real property and personal property.

  - Real Property (realty or real estate): includes land and property that is permanently attached to it.

  - Personal Property (chattel): property that is not attached to the land.

Personal Property

- Personal and real property can be either tangible or intangible.

  - Tangible Property: includes physically defined property.

  - Intangible Property: represents rights that cannot be reduced to physical form.

Property Ownership

- The legal term for property ownership rights is title. Title is thought of as a bundle of rights related to the property.
- Fee Simple: absolute ownership entitling the property owner to possess, use, or dispose of the property as the owner chooses.

Property Ownership: Concurrent Ownership

- **Tenancy in Common**: co-ownership of property in which each party owns an undivided interest in the whole property.
  - Devise: _____
  - Transfer: _____
  - Ownership Interest: _____
  - Creditor's Claims: _____
  - Partition: _____
  - Wording: _____

Property Ownership: Concurrent Ownership

- **Joint Tenancy With Right of Survivorship**: when one of the joint tenants dies, his/her interest passes equally to the surviving joint tenant(s).
  - Devise: _____
  - Transfer: _____
  - Creditor's Claims: _____
  - Advantage: _____
  - Partition: _____
  - Wording: _____

Property Ownership: Concurrent Ownership

- **Tenancy by the Entirety**: a form of co-ownership of property that can be used only by married couples.
  - Devise: _____
  - Transfer: _____
  - Creditor's Claims: _____
  - Divorce: _____
  - Wording: _____

Florida's Homestead Law

- The Florida Constitution protects homestead property from a forced sale to a creditor.
- Requirements:
  - One's principal place of residence up to one-half acre within a municipality and up to 160 contiguous acres in any county in Florida.
  - Some exceptions:
    - Federal tax lien;
    - Assessments;
    - Obligations contracted for labor performed on the property.

Acquiring an Ownership Interest in Personal Property

- Purchase

- Possession

- Production

- Confusion

- Gift
  - Intent
  - Delivery
  - Acceptance

Mislaid, Lost, or Abandoned Personal Property

- Mislaid Property: property is mislaid when it is intentionally put somewhere, but then forgotten.
- Lost Property: property is considered lost if the owner has unknowingly or accidentally left it somewhere or dropped it somewhere.
- Abandoned Property: property is classified as abandoned if (1) an owner discards the property with the intent to relinquish his or her rights to it or (2) an owner of mislaid or lost property gives up any further attempts to locate it.

Chapter 49
Real Property

Chapter 49

Real Property

Real Property Elements

- Real property consists of:
  - Land and everything permanently attached to it;
  - Water rights;
  - Subsurface rights;
  - Air rights;
  - Plant life and Vegetation; and
  - Fixtures.

Ownership of Real Property

- Fee Simple Absolute: a type of ownership of real property that grants the owner the fullest bundle of legal rights that a person can hold in real property.
- Fee Simple Defeasible: a type of ownership of real property that grants the owner all the incidents of a fee simple absolute except that it may be taken away if a specified condition occurs or does not occur.
- Life Estate: an interest in real property that lasts for the life of a specified person. The person who has the life estate interest is known as the life tenant.

Non-Possessory Interests

- License: a revocable right or privilege to come onto the land of another.

- Easement: a limited right to use another person's land for a specific purpose.
  - Easement Appurtenant

  - Easement in Gross

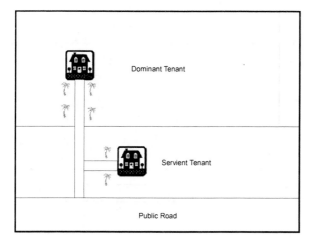

Non-Possessory Interests

- Profit: the right to obtain a possessory interest in some aspect of another's land, such as crops, timber, or minerals.

Non-Possessory Interests

- Creation of easements and profits:
  - Deed, Will, Contract
  - Implication – grantor conveys a portion of the real estate he owns or when he divides a larger tract among separate grantees
  - Necessity – landlocked property.
  - Prescription – similar to adverse possession.

Transfer of Real Property

- Title to real property may be transferred by sale, gift, will, inheritance, and adverse possession. Deeds are used to convey real property by sale or gift.
- A valid deed must be in writing and must, at the minimum, contain:
  - the names of the buyer and seller;
  - words of conveyance;
  - a precise, legally sufficient description of the land;
  - the grantor's signature; and
  - the deed must be delivered to the grantee.

Transfer of Real Property

- Types of deeds:
  - Warranty Deed: a deed in which the grantor warrants good, clear title to the grantee. The usual covenants are possession, quiet enjoyment, right to convey, freedom from encumbrances, and defense of title to all claims.
  - Quit-Claim Deed: a deed containing no warranty of title.
- Other types of deeds:
  - Sheriff's (Foreclosure) Deed
  - Special Warranty Deed
  - Personal Representative's Deed
  - Trustee's Deed

Transfer of Real Property

- The sale of real property generally involves the following:
  - Listing the property for sale by owner or through the use of real estate agent.
  - Contract of sale, which must be in writing to be enforceable.
  - Title search, generally performed to determine if the grantor has marketable title.
  - Mortgage, when money is borrowed to purchase the property.
  - At closing, delivery of the deed to the buyer, who pays the purchase price. The money is then disbursed.

Seller's Duties

- Implied Warranty of Habitability: most states hold that an implied warranty accompanies the sale of a new home.
  - The warranty provides that the house has been constructed in a workmanlike manner and is fit for human habitation.

Seller's Duties

- Duty to Disclose: in most jurisdictions, a seller must disclose:
  - any known defect that materially affects the value of the property, which the buyer could not reasonably discover.

Adverse Possession

- In most states, a person who wrongfully possesses someone else's property obtains title to that property if certain statutory requirements are met.
- The occupation must be:
  - Actual and Exclusive
  - Open, Visible, and Notorious
  - Continuous and Peaceful
  - Hostile and Adverse

Eminent Domain

- The right of the federal and state governments, as well some other entities with governmental powers, to take privately owned real property for the public benefit.
  - The Fifth Amendment to the U.S. Constitution requires that the owner be compensated for the property taken.
  - The amount awarded is generally the property's fair market value before the taking occurred.

Restrictions on Land-Use Rights

- The owner's right to use his/her land is now usually subject to many governmental controls, including zoning and building codes.
- Zoning is a legislative action, usually at the municipal level. It regulates the use of property, including the types of construction permitted within different zoning districts.

Restrictions on Land-Use Rights

- Private restrictions called restrictive covenants can be placed in deeds and subdivision plans as long as they are not unlawful or otherwise contrary to public policy.

Chapter 49
Landlord-Tenant

Chapter 49

Landlord-Tenant Relationships

Landlord-Tenant

- The owner of the real property is the landlord, who puts possession of the real property in the hands of the tenant.

Leasehold Estates

- There are four types of leasehold estates:
  - Tenancy for Years: a leasehold estate for a specified period of time.
    - Termination: _____
  - Periodic Tenancy: a leasehold estate for a period determined by the frequency of rent payments.
    - Termination: _____

Leasehold Estates

- Tenancy at Will: a leasehold estate for as long as both parties agree.
  - Termination:_____
- Tenancy at Sufferance: tenancy continues after the lease has expired.
  - Termination: _____

The Lease Agreement

- A lease agreement should:
  - express an intent to establish a landlord-tenant relationship;
  - provide for transfer of possession of the property to the tenant at the beginning of the lease;
  - provide for the reversion of possession of the property to the landlord at the end of the lease's term;
  - describe the property;
  - clearly indicate the length of the lease term, the amount of rent due, and how and when rent is to be paid; and
  - provide for other covenants.

The Lease Agreement

- Many state laws make it illegal for:
  - a lease to require the tenant to pay the landlord's attorneys' fees;
  - a landlord to rent a structure that is in disrepair or not in compliance with building codes;
  - a landlord to lease for an illegal purpose; or
  - a landlord to refuse to lease based on race, color, religion, national origin, sex, or handicap.

The Lease Agreement

- Unconscionability: a lease containing one or more material, unconscionable terms may be void as a matter of law.

Landlord's Duty to Deliver Possession

- The landlord's duty is to deliver possession of the premises at the start of the tenancy.

Quiet Enjoyment

- Covenant of Quiet Enjoyment: the law implies a covenant of quiet enjoyment in all leases.
  - Under this covenant, the landlord may not interfere with the tenant's quiet and peaceful possession, use, and enjoyment of the leased premises.

Eviction

- The most common inference with the covenant of quiet enjoyment is an eviction. Eviction is an act that forces a tenant to abandon the premises.
  - Constructive eviction occurs when the landlord wrongfully causes the leased premises to become unfit for its intended use.
  - Retaliatory eviction occurs when the landlord evicts a tenant for complaining to the appropriate authorities about the improper condition of the leased premises.

Tenant's Implied Covenants to Landlord

- The tenant may not create a nuisance that substantially interferes with others' quiet enjoyment of their own property rights.
- The tenant is obligated not to commit waste by abusing or destroying the leased property.
- The tenant is responsible for all damages to the premises caused by the tenant or tenant's guests and invitees, except for ordinary wear and tear.

Maintenance of Rented Property

- Common Areas: the landlord must maintain all areas used by or accessible to all tenants, such as hallways, stairs, elevators, and laundry rooms.

8/11/2015

Maintenance of Rented Property

- Implied Warranty of Habitability: the courts of many jurisdictions hold that an implied warranty of habitability applies to residential leases for their duration.
  - This warranty provides that the leased premises must be fit, safe, and suitable for ordinary residential use.

Maintenance of Rented Property

- Tenant's Remedies: if the landlord's failure to maintain or repair the leased premises affects the tenant's use or enjoyment of the premises, the tenant may:
  - withhold rent;
  - repair and deduct the cost of repair from rent due;
  - cancel the lease; or
  - sue for the lost use of the premises and/or the cost of repair.

Rent

- Rent is the compensation paid by the tenant to the landlord for the use of the premises.

5

Rent Issues

- Security Deposit: tenants often are required to pay a security deposit to the landlord.
- Late Charges: a landlord may also assess a penalty for late payment of rent.
- Rent Escalation: unless the lease otherwise provides, rent may not be increased during the lease term.

Rent Issues

- Landlord's Remedies: if a tenant fails to pay rent, the landlord may do one or more of the following:
  - secure a lien on the tenant's personal property;
  - subject to any duty to mitigate, sue for the unpaid rent and the costs incurred collecting it; or
  - retake possession of the property by legal means.

Premises Liability

- Tenant's Liability: a tenant is generally liable for injuries occurring within the premises she is leasing, whether that is an apartment, a store, or otherwise.
  - For example, if a tenant allows grease to accumulate on a kitchen floor and a guest slips and falls, the tenant is liable.
- Generally, a tenant is not liable for injuries occurring in common areas over which he has no control (for example, exterior sidewalks).
- A landlord may be liable if a tenant's guest slips and falls because the common stairs in the building have loose steps.

Premises Liability

- Landlord's Liability: Common Law Rules: historically, a landlord was responsible for injuries on the premises only in limited circumstances:
  - Latent Defects: if the landlord knows of a dangerous condition on the property and realizes the tenant will not notice it, the landlord is responsible for any injuries.
  - Common Areas: the landlord is usually responsible for maintaining the common areas.
  - Negligent Repairs: if the landlord volunteers to make repairs (even in areas where the landlord has no duty to make repairs) and does the work poorly, the landlord is responsible.
  - Public Use: if the premises are being used for a public purpose, the landlord, generally, must repair any dangerous defects (the tenant is probably responsible as well).

Premises Liability

- Modern Trend
  - State legislatures and courts are discarding the common law rules and holding landlords liable under negligence laws.
  - In many states, a landlord must use reasonable care to maintain safe premises and will be liable for foreseeable harm.

Landlord's Liability for Crime

- Landlords may be liable to tenants or their guests for criminal attacks that occur on the premises.
- Courts typically look at the following four factors in determining whether a landlord will be liable for a criminal attack:
  - Nature of the crime;
  - Reasonable person standard;
  - Foreseeability; and
  - Crime in the area.

Transfer of Landlord's Interest

- Landlord's may sell, gift, devise, or otherwise transfer their interests in the leased property.

Transfer of Tenant's Interest

- Assuming that the terms of the lease allow for the tenant to transfer possession of the leased premises, a tenant may transfer his or her interest in leased property as follows:
  - Assignment: if a tenant transfers all of his or her interest under a lease, it is an assignment.
  - Sublease: if a tenant transfers only some of his or her rights under the lease, it is a sublease.

Terminating the Lease

- Expiration and Surrender: most leases terminate when their term ends. The tenant then surrenders the property to the landlord, who retakes possession of the property or delivers possession to another tenant.
- Release and Merger: A lease may also give the tenant the opportunity to purchase the property at or before the end of the lease. If the tenant does so, she is released from any more obligations under the lease.

Chapter 36
Sole Proprietorships and Franchises

Chapter 36

Sole Proprietorships and Franchises

Starting a Business

- To begin a business, entrepreneurs must select a form of organization.
- The correct form of business organization can reduce taxes, reduce liability, and reduce conflict.
- If an entrepreneur does not make a choice for himself/herself, the law will automatically select a default option.

Sole Proprietorships

- The sole proprietorship is merely an extension of its only owner, the sole proprietor.
- The sole proprietorship is not a legal entity.
  - Formation:
    - Very easily and inexpensively.

Sole Proprietorships

- Advantages:
  - the ease and low cost to form;

  - the proprietor receives all of the profits;

  - the owner has the maximum degree of control over business decisions; and

  - the sole proprietorship can be easily transferred or sold if and when the owner desires to do so.

Sole Proprietorships

- Disadvantages:
  - the proprietor has unlimited liability for any losses or liabilities incurred by the entity;

  - the entity will not survive the proprietor's death, disability, or retirement; and

  - the proprietor may only raise capital for the business out of his personal funds and from loans others are willing to make based on his personal liability.

Franchises

- A contractual relationship where the owner of a trademark, trade name, commercial symbols, operation, system, process, or copyright (the franchisor) allows another person or entity (the franchisee) to use that property, operation, process, or system.

Franchises

- Advantages to Franchising:
  - The franchisor can reach new markets while the franchisee absorbs much of the risk.

  - The franchisee has access to the franchisor's knowledge and resources.

  - Consumers are assured of uniform product quality.

Franchises

- Disadvantages to Franchising:

  - Must meet the franchisor's standards or risk losing the franchise.

  - Little control over the business.

Franchises

- Types of Franchises:
  - Distributorship Franchise: the franchisor manufactures a product and licenses a retail franchisee to distribute the product to the public.
  - Chain Store Franchise: the franchisor licenses the franchisee to make and sell its products or distribute services to the public from a retail outlet serving an exclusive territory.
  - Manufacturing or Processing Plant: the franchisor provides a secret formula or process to the franchisee. The franchisee manufactures the product and distributes it to retail dealers.

Franchise Laws

- The Automobile Dealers' Franchise Act protects automobile dealership franchisees whose franchisors impose unreasonable demands and then terminate the franchise because of the franchisee's failure to satisfy them.
- The Petroleum Marketing Practices Act prescribes the grounds and conditions under which a franchisor may terminate or decline to renew a gas station's franchise.

Franchise Laws

- The Federal Trade Commission (FTC) is the federal regulatory authority that oversees the regulation of franchisors.
- The FTC requires franchisors to disclose material facts that a prospective franchisee needs in order to make an informed decision whether to purchase a franchise.

Franchise Agreement

- Typically, the following are a few of the issues addressed in the Franchise Agreement:
  - Payment for the Franchise
    - Royalties
  - Business Premises
  - Location
  - Quality Controls
  - Price Controls
  - Duration

Franchise Termination

- Most franchise agreements provide that termination must be "for cause."

  - If a franchisor terminates a franchise agreement without just cause, the franchisee can sue the franchisor for wrongful termination.

_____

_____

_____

_____

_____

_____

_____

Chapter 37
Partnerships

Chapter 37

Partnerships, Limited Partnerships, Limited Liability
Partnerships, Limited Liability Limited Partnerships

Partnerships

- Partnerships are largely governed by statutory law.
- The Uniform Partnership Act (UPA) of 1994, with the 1997 amendments (the Revised Uniform Partnership Act (RUPA)), is a model partnership statute drafted by the National Conference of Commissioners on Uniform State Laws.
- Florida has adopted RUPA.

General Partnerships

- Definition:
  - An association of two or more persons;

  - carrying on a business;

  - as co-owners;

  - for profit.

General Partnerships

- Advantages:
  - Most states state that the partnership is an entity distinct from its partners;
  - partnerships are easy and inexpensive to form;
    - Documents that may be filed with the Secretary of State:_____
    _____
  - the partners share all of the profits; and
  - the partners may raise capital for the business out of their collective personal funds and from loans others are willing to make based on their collective or individual liability.

General Partnerships

- Disadvantages:
  - partners may have personal liability for partnership obligations; and
  - partners are jointly and severally liable for partnership obligations.

General Partnerships

- Partnership Agreement:
  - The partnership's name.

  - A description of the partnership's business.

  - A listing of the present partners.

  - A statement of the contributions made and/or to be made by the present partners.

General Partnerships

- Partnership Agreement continued:
  - A method for dividing profits and losses.
  - Withdrawal of a partner or addition of a partner.
  - Methods of transferring a partnership interest.
  - Partnership's term of duration:
    - Partnership for a term:

      _____.

    - Partnership at will:

      _____.

General Partnerships

- Unless the partnership agrees otherwise, under RUPA:
  - All partners have equal rights in the management and a duty to help manage the partnership;
  - Each partner has an equal vote; and
  - Any partnership act not in the ordinary course of business must be approved by all partners.
    - For example, the decision of a small accounting partnership in St. Pete to open a second office in Tampa would require a unanimous vote of the partners.

General Partnerships

- Assignment of Partnership Interest: A partner may voluntarily assign his interest in the partnership to a third party.
- Lien on Partnership Interest: A partner's interest may also be subject to a judgment creditor's lien.

General Partnerships

- Compensation: Generally, partners do not receive a salary for any work they do for the benefit of the partnership.
  - Profits

  - Losses

General Partnerships

- Partnership Taxation:
  - A partnership must file an annual information return, but it does not pay income tax.
  - Instead, it "passes through" any profits or losses to its partners.

General Partnerships

- Partnership books and records must be kept accessible to all partners.
- Each partner has the right to receive full and complete information concerning all aspects of the partnership business.
- Every partner, whether active or inactive, is entitled to inspect all books and records and may copy any materials.

General Partnerships

- Property belongs to the partnership if the property:
  - is acquired with partnership funds; and
  - is transferred to the partnership in its name.

General Partnerships

- Fiduciary duties: partners stand in a fiduciary relationship to one another.
- Some of the duties among partners are: Duty of Loyalty and Duty of Care.

Partnerships

- Duty of Loyalty: a duty that a partner owes not to act adversely to the interests of the partnership.
- Partners breach their duty of loyalty if they:
  - self-deal without permission;
  - compete with the partnership without permission;
  - make secret profits from the partnership business;
  - disclose confidential partnership information; or
  - misuse partnership property.

Partnerships

- Duty of Care: the obligation partners owe to use the same level of care and skill that a reasonable person in the same position would use in the same circumstances.

Limited Partnerships

- Two types of partners:
  - General partners, who invest capital, manage the business, share in its profits, and are personally liable for partnership debts; and
  - Limited partners, who invest capital and share profits, but do not participate in management and are not personally liable for partnership debts beyond their capital contribution.

Limited Partnerships

- Forming an LP requires complying with relevant statutes, preparing a certificate of limited partnership, and filing it with the Secretary of State.
- Under the Uniform Limited Partnership Act (ULPA 2001), information that the certificate of limited partnership must contain:
  - name of the limited partnership;
  - address of the principal place of business;
  - name and address of the registered agent;
  - name and address of each general partner; and
  - whether it is a limited partnership or an LLLP.

Limited Partnerships
- Rights and Liabilities Shared by General and Limited Partners:
  - Capital Contributions: a partner may contribute any property or other benefit to the limited partnership such as:

    _____
    _____
    _____

  - Share of Profits and Losses: under the ULPA, profits and losses are shared on the basis of the value of each partner's capital contribution (unless there's a written agreement stating otherwise).

_____
_____
_____
_____
_____
_____
_____

Limited Partnerships

- Rights and Liabilities Shared by General and Limited Partners:
  - Voting Rights: the ULPA requires few actions to be approved by all of the partners.
  - Admission of New Partners: the ULPA's default rule is that no new partner may be admitted unless each partner consents to the admission.

_____
_____
_____
_____
_____
_____
_____

Limited Partnerships

- Additional Rights of General Partners
  - The general partner has the same right to manage as a partner in a general partnership.
  - Compensation?

_____
_____
_____
_____
_____
_____

Limited Partnerships

- Liability of the General Partner: a general partner's liability is unlimited personal liability for the debts and obligations of the limited partnership.
- Fiduciary Duties?

Limited Partnerships

- Additional Rights of Limited Partners
  - They have the right to be informed about the partnership affairs.
  - A limited partner may inspect and copy a list of the partners, tax returns, partnership agreements, information concerning contributions by partners, and the certificate of limited partnership.

Limited Partnerships

- Liability of the Limited Partner: A limited partner's liability is limited to the amount of his capital contribution.
- Fiduciary Duties?

Limited Liability Partnerships

- A form of partnership that has elected to obtain limited liability for its partners.
- The LLP is designed for professionals who historically have done business as partners.
- LLP's enjoy the flow-through tax benefit of other types of partnerships.
  - All profits and losses are reported on the individual partners' income tax returns.

_____

_____

_____

_____

_____

_____

_____

Limited Liability Limited Partnerships

- A limited liability limited partnership (LLLP) is a form of limited partnership.

_____

_____

_____

_____

_____

_____

_____

Chapter 38
Limited Liability Companies

Chapter 38

Limited Liability Companies

Limited Liability Companies

- A business entity that combines the most favorable attributes of general partnerships, limited partnerships, and corporations.
- Every state and the District of Columbia have adopted an LLC statute.
- The National Commissioners on Uniform State Laws has adopted the Revised Uniform Limited Liability Company Act of 2006 (RULLCA).

Limited Liability Companies

- Advantages
  - Member's (the owners) enjoy limited personal liability;

  - Flexibility in management and operations; and

  - Less restrictive in ownership.

Limited Liability Companies

- Disadvantages
  - Non-uniform state LLC statutes create uncertainty.

Limited Liability Companies

- Formation: an LLC is formed by delivering articles of organization to the Secretary of State for filing.
- The Florida Statutes requires the articles of organization to set forth:
  - The name of the LLC;
  - The mailing address and street address of the LLC's principal office;
  - The name and address of the registered agent along with a signed written statement;
  - Any other matters the members elect to include in the articles of organization; and
  - To be executed by at least one member or the authorized representative of a member.

Limited Liability Companies

- Operating Agreement: agreement of the members covering topics such as:
  - Management of the LLC;
  - Sharing of profits;
  - Withdrawal from the LLC;
  - Transferring membership interests; and
  - Other aspects of the LLC's operation.

Limited Liability Companies

- Taxation
  - Multi-member LLC: _____
  _____
  - Single-member LLC: _____
  _____

Limited Liability Companies

- Member's Liabilities
  - A member's liability is usually limited to her/his capital contribution to the LLC.
    - Exceptions:
      - Personal guarantee.
      - Piercing the corporate veil.

Limited Liability Companies

- Management: LLC's are typically either member-managed or manager-managed.
  - In a member-managed LLC, all members participate in the management.
  - In a manager-managed LLC, only the designated manager(s) have authority to bind the LLC to contracts.

Limited Liability Companies

- Duties
  - Each manager in a manager-managed LLC and each member in a member-managed LLC is a fiduciary of the LLC and its members.

Limited Liability Companies

- Distributions to Member's
  - An important right to a member of an LLC is the right to receive distributions from the LLC.

Limited Liability Companies

- Member's Ownership Interest
  - A member has limited ability to sell or transfer his/her rights in the LLC.
  - The operating agreement may provide that a transferee becomes a member of the LLC. If this is the case, the transferee then has the powers, rights, and liabilities of the transferring member.
  - A personal creditor of a member may obtain a charging order.

Chapter 39
Corporations

Chapter 39

Corporations

Corporations

- Definition: an artificial being created by operation of law, with an existence separate from the individuals who own and operate it.
  - Other Advantages:
    - Limited liability;
    - Centralized management;
    - Ability to raise capital; and
    - Transferability of shares.

Corporations

- Disadvantages
  - Expense;

  - Formalities; and

  - Regulations.

Corporations

- Corporations are treated as artificial persons that can:
  - sue or be sued in the corporations' own name;

  - hold title to and transfer property; and

  - enter into and enforce contracts.

Piercing The Corporate Veil

- If a court "pierces the corporate veil," the corporate entity is disregarded and the wrongdoers can be sued individually.
- The following factors may persuade a court to pierce the corporate veil:
  - the corporation was created never to make a profit or had insufficient capital at the time of its formation;
  - the corporation does not observe statutorily-required corporate formalities; and
  - personal and corporate interests are commingled.

Corporate Taxation

- Corporate profits are taxable. Corporations may do one of two things with corporate profits – retain them or pass them on to shareholders in the form of dividends.
  - Dividends: corporate profits distributed to shareholders in proportion to their shares held.
  - Retained earnings: corporate profits that are not distributed.

Constitutional Rights

- A corporation is a "person" for purposes of most rights guaranteed by the U.S. Constitution; however, corporations do not enjoy:

  - Fifth Amendment protection against self-incrimination; or

  - Privileges and Immunities Clause protection.

Corporate Promoter

- Promoter: a person who conceives of, organizes, and begins the corporation and takes the steps of establishing the corporation, including:
  - issuing a prospectus;
  - finding initial investors to finance the corporation;
  - making contracts; and
  - securing a corporate charter.

Corporate Promoter

- Promoters' Contracts include leases, sales contracts, contracts to purchase real or personal property, employment contracts, etc. Promoters' liability and the liability of the corporation on these contracts follow these rules:
  - If the corporation never comes into existence, the promoters have _____ liability on the contract unless the third party _____.
  - If the corporation is formed, it becomes liable on a promoter's contract only if it _____.
  - Even if the corporation agrees to be bound to the contract, the promoter remains liable on the contract unless the parties enter in a _____.

Incorporation

- First step is to select a state of incorporation. A corporation can be incorporated in only one state even though it can do business in all other states in which it qualifies to do business.
- Articles of Incorporation: the basic governing document of the corporation.
- The State of Florida requires the following information to be contained in the Articles of Incorporation:
  - the name of the corporation;
  - principal place of business and mailing address, if different, of the corporation;
  - capital structure;
  - name and address of registered agent;
  - the name and address of the incorporator; and
  - signature of the incorporator.

Incorporation

- First Organizational Meeting: the incorporators call a meeting of the initial board of directors.
  - Adoption of bylaws.
  - Elect corporate officers.
  - Transact any other such business as may come before the meeting.

Equity Securities

- Stock: An equity security that represents the purchase of a share of ownership in a corporation by a shareholder.
- There are two classes of equity stock: common shares and preferred shares.

Common Stock

- Securities which represent an ownership interest in a corporation.
- Common stockholders vote for directors and on other fundamental corporate matters and have limited liability.
- Common stock shares are the last to receive dividends and to receive asset distribution upon the corporation's dissolution.

Preferred Stock

- The class of shares that takes priority over common shares as to:

  - distribution of dividends; and

  - distribution upon liquidation.

Corporate Powers

- The implied powers of a corporation are powers beyond the express powers that allow a corporation to accomplish its corporate purpose.
  - A corporation has the implied power to open a bank account.

  - A corporation has the implied power to reimburse its employees for expenses.

Corporations

- Domestic Corporation: A corporation incorporated in a given state and doing business in that same state.

- Foreign Corporation: A corporation doing business in a given state, but incorporated in another state.

Corporations

- Public Corporation: A corporation formed by a government to serve some public purpose.
- Publicly-Held Corporation: A corporation whose shares are sold to and held by, or on behalf of, the general public, and are traded on a public exchange.
  - Facebook, Inc., eBay, Inc., Starbucks Corporation, Ford Motor Company are examples.
- Non-Profit Corporation: A corporation formed, in many cases, for charitable, educational, religious, or similar purposes, and organized and operated without the goal of making a profit.

Corporations

- Close Corporation (a.k.a. "closely-held corporation"): A privately-held corporation with a small number of shareholders, often members of the same family.
  - Management resembles that of a sole proprietorship or partnership, with one or a few of the firm's owners also holding positions as officers and directors.
  - Transfer restrictions: close corporations often require a shareholder who wishes to exit the corporation to sell their shares to the other existing shareholders, or at least offer them or the corporation a right of first refusal.

Corporations

- S-Corporation: a corporation organized to meet certain IRS Code requirements and thus qualify for special federal income tax treatment.

- The income of a S-corporation is taxed only at the individual shareholder level.

Corporations

- Special Types of For-Profit Corporations in Florida:
  - The Benefit Corporation (B Corporation): statutory purpose is to pursue a "general public benefit," defined as "a material, positive effect on society and the environment, taken as a whole..."
  - The Social Purpose Corporation (SP Corporation): the statutory purpose is to create a "public benefit" (the word "general" is deliberately omitted).
- The intent of the new legislation is to accommodate entrepreneurs and investors who want a for-profit corporation that may engage in a substantial socially beneficial activities to an extent beyond what may be allowed for traditional corporations.

Chapter 40
Shareholders, Directors, and Officers

Chapter 40

Shareholders, Directors and Officers

Shareholders

- Owners of the shares of stock issued by the corporation and, therefore, the owners of the corporation.

Shareholders

- Limited Liability of Shareholders: shareholders are generally not personally liable for the obligations of the corporation.
  - When might shareholders be personally liable for corporation obligations?
  - When the court "pierces the corporate veil."

Shareholder Approval

- Generally, shareholders must approve fundamental corporate changes before the changes can be implemented, such as:
  - amendments to the articles of incorporation or by-laws;
  - a merger or dissolution of the corporation;

Shareholder Approval

- an increase in the number of shares of stock that the corporation is authorized to issue; and
- a sale of all or substantially all of the corporation's assets.
  - Principal test:

    _____ .

Shareholder Meetings

- Annual shareholders' meetings are held to elect directors, choose an independent auditor, and take other actions.
- Special shareholders' meetings may be called by the board of director to consider important or emergency issues, such as a merger.

Shareholder Meetings

- The president or chairman of the board usually presides and the minutes are kept by the secretary of the corporation.
- In order for votes recorded at a shareholders' meeting to be effective, there must be a quorum present – that is, there must be enough shareholders and others holding proxies present to represent at least 50 percent of the corporation's voting stock.

Shareholders' Shares

- Stock Certificate: a certificate issued by a corporation that evidences ownership of a specified number of shares of the corporation and all rights attached thereto.
- Preemptive Right: existing shareholders may have the right to preempt, or come ahead, of other purchasers of stock of the same class in order to protect their percentage interest in, or control of, the corporation.

Dividends

- A distribution of corporate profits or income, ordered by the directors, and paid to shareholders in proportion to their respective shares in the corporation.

Shareholders' Inspection Rights

- Shareholders are entitled to inspect the corporation's books and records:
  - for a proper purpose;
  - in person or through an agent (attorney, accountant, or other authorized assistant); and
  - provided that the request is made in advance.

Shareholders' Transfer Rights

- Generally, shareholders have the right to transfer their shares. However, sometimes shareholders may want to restrict the ability of other shareholders to transfer their shares to parties who are not currently shareholders. Two of these restrictive methods:
- Right of first refusal: _____

  _____.
- Buy-and-sell agreement: _____

  _____.

Shareholder Derivative Lawsuit

- Shareholder Derivative Suit: a lawsuit brought by one or more shareholders on behalf of the corporation for the benefit of the corporation.
  - The lawsuit is brought against the corporation's directors or others for injury to the corporation.

Directors

- A corporation is governed by a board of directors who are:
  - elected by the corporation's shareholders,
  - to serve for a period of time,
  - compensated as provided for in the articles or by-laws,
  - entitled to: receive reasonable notice of and to participate in all board meetings, inspect all corporate books and records, and, in most jurisdictions, to be indemnified by the corporation for any judgment entered against them,
  - responsible for: declaring and paying corporate dividends, authorizing major corporate decisions, appointing, supervising, and removing corporate officers and managerial employees, and deciding whether to issue stock or bonds.

Directors

- Committees: although board members cannot delegate their responsibilities and duties, committees of board members may be designated to perform a number of board-type activities under the general supervision of the whole board.
- Board of directors are typically composed of inside and outside directors.

Officers

- Persons named and hired by the board of directors to supervise the day-to-day operations of the corporation.
- Designation of the various offices and the duties of each office are set forth in the bylaws.
- Generally, the officers are the president, one or more vice presidents, the secretary, and the treasurer.

Duty of Care

- Directors and officers are expected to:
  - act in good faith in performing their duties;
  - exercise the care that an ordinarily prudent person would exercise in similar circumstances; and
  - act in the best interest of the corporation.

Duty of Care

- Directors and officers must do what is necessary to become and stay informed on important corporate matters. In addition, directors are expected to:
  - make reasonable decisions;
  - exercise reasonable supervision over corporate officers and employees; and
  - attend and participate in board meetings.

Duty of Loyalty

- Directors and officers are required to place the corporation's best interest ahead of their personal interests when the two do not coincide. As a general rule, directors and officers may not:
  - use corporate funds or confidential information for their own personal gain;
  - engage in self-dealing;
  - compete with the corporation, or otherwise take personal advantage of a corporate opportunity;

Duty of Loyalty

- have an interest that conflicts with the interest of the corporation;
- engage in insider trading;
- authorize corporate transactions detrimental to minority shareholders without prior shareholder approval; or
- sell control of the corporation without prior shareholder approval.

Sarbanes-Oxley Act

- In response to the business and accounting scandals, Congress enacted the Sarbanes-Oxley Act of 2002 (SOX). The Act established rules regarding corporate governance. Some of the major provisions:
  - CEO and CFO certification: the CEO and chief financial officer (CFO) of a public company must file a statement accompanying each annual and quarterly report called the CEO and CFO certification. This statement certifies that the signing officer has reviewed the report; that, based on the officer's knowledge, the report does not contain any untrue statement of a material fact or omit to state a material fact that would make the statement misleading. A knowing and willful violation is punishable by up to 20 years in prison a monetary fine.
  - Reimbursement of bonuses and incentive pay: if a public company is required to restate its financial statements because of material noncompliance with financial reporting requirements, the CEO and CFO must reimburse the company for any bonuses, incentive pay, or securities trading profits made because of the noncompliance.

Business Judgment Rule

- Directors and officers are immune from personal liability for actions that result in harm to the corporation as long as:
  - the directors and officers acted
    - in good faith,
    - in the best interest of the corporation, and
    - with the due care, and
  - the actions taken were within
    - the corporation's power to act, and
    - the directors' and officers' authority.

Chapter 51
Estate Planning

Chapter 51

Wills, Trusts, and Elder Law

Estate Planning

• Estate planning is the popular name for the process of planning for the transfer of a person's estate before or after death.

Wills

• A will is an instrument, executed by a testator (male) or a testatrix (female) stating how that person's estate is to be distributed after death.

Wills

- Types of Gifts:
  - Devise: a gift of real estate.
  - Bequest (also called legacy): a gift of personal property or money.

Wills

- Gifts in a will can be specific, general, or residuary.
  - Specific Gifts are of specifically named pieces of property.
  - General Gifts do not identify the specific property from which the gift is to be made (such as a cash amount that can come from any source in the decedent's estate).
  - Residuary Gifts are established by a residuary clause in the will.

Wills

- For a will to be valid, it must meet the following requirements:
  - Testamentary Capacity: the testator must have been of legal age and sound mind when the will was made.
  - To have testamentary capacity, the testator must:
    - intend the document to be his last will;
    - comprehend the kind and character of the property being distributed by the will; and
    - comprehend and remember the "natural objects of his bounty."

Wills

- Requirements for a valid will continued:
  - Writing Requirement: generally, wills must be in writing to be valid.
    - Holographic Will: a will that is entirely handwritten and signed by the testator.
    - Nuncupative Will: an oral will made before witnesses.
  - Testator's Signature: the testator's signature must appear on the face of the will.
  - Attestation by Witnesses: wills must be attested to by mentally competent witnesses.

Estate Planning
Per Stirpes vs. Per Capita

TWO WAYS TO LEAVE ESTATE TO CHILDREN

Per Stirpes

Per Capita

Wills

- Per stirpes: each surviving descendant divides the share that his or her parent would have taken if the parent would have survived. If the parent is still living, they receive nothing.

- Per capita: each person takes an equal share.

Per Stirpes Example

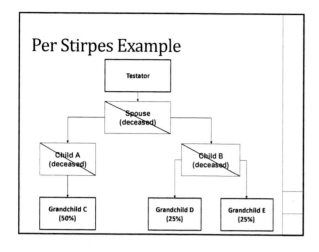

Per Capita Example

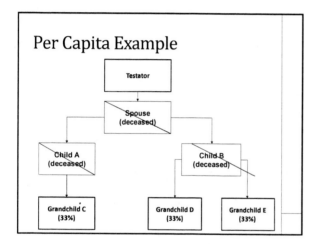

Wills

- Codicil: the legal way to change an existing will.

  - A codicil is a separate document that must be executed with the same formalities as a will.

Wills

- Revocation:
  - Physical Act: intentionally burning, tearing, canceling or otherwise destroying the will or directing another to do so in the testator's presence.
  - Subsequent Writing: intentionally making a new will or amending or revoking any or all of a will by means of a codicil.
  - Operation of Law: due to marriage, divorce, annulment, or the birth of one or more children after the will was executed.

Probate

- The legal process required to establish the validity of a will and to administer the decedent's estate.
- Types of probate:
  - Informal Probate/Summary Administration: most states allow the assets of smaller estates to be distributed without formal probate proceedings.
  - Formal Probate/Formal Administration: for larger estates and for smaller estates that require the appointment of a guardian, the probate court generally supervises every aspect of the payment of the decedent's surviving obligations and the distribution of the decedent's assets.

Probate

- Non-Probate Assets:
  - Property owned by husband and wife as tenants by the entirety.

  - A life insurance policy, annuity, or IRA account that is payable to a specific beneficiary.

Intestacy

- When a person dies without leaving a valid will, he is said to have died intestate.
- In such cases, the deceased's property passes according to law, rather than according to his wishes.
- Florida:
  - If the decedent is married and there are no surviving descendants of the decedent, the entire intestate estate passes to _____.
  - If the married decedent is survived by one or more descendants, all of whom are also descendants of the surviving spouse, and the surviving spouse has no other descendant, the entire intestate estate passes to _____.
  - If there are one or more surviving descendants of the decedent who are not lineal descendants of the surviving spouse, _____ of the intestate estate goes to _____.
  - If there are one or more surviving descendants of the decedent, all of whom are also descendants of the surviving spouse, and the surviving spouse has one or more descendants who are not descendants of the decedent, _____ of the intestate estate goes to _____.

Trusts

- A trust is a legal arrangement under which one person (the grantor) delivers and transfers legal title to property to another person (the trustee) to be held and used for the benefit of a third person (the beneficiary).
- Types of Trusts:
  - Testamentary Trust: a testamentary trust is created by will. The trust comes into existence when the settlor dies.
  - Living Trust: grantor creates the trust during his/her life.

Trusts

- Types of Trusts continued:
  - Charitable Trust: a trust in which the property held by a trustee must be used for a charitable purpose, such as the advancement of health, education, or religion.
  - Totten Trust: a trust created by the deposit of a person's own money in his or her own name as trustee for another.

Estate Administration

- Personal Representative: a person designated by the decedent's will or by a court to administer a decedent's estate.
- Duties of the Personal Representative include:
  - identifying, gathering, safeguarding, and inventorying the decedent's assets, and having them appraised, as necessary;
  - managing the estate's assets and preventing them from being wasted or unnecessarily depleted;
  - receiving and paying valid claims of the decedent's creditors and objecting to improper claims and defending suits brought on such claims;

Estate Administration

- Duties of Personal Representative continued:
  - paying or arranging for payment of income, estate, and inheritance taxes due;
  - distributing the remaining assets of the estate to the decedent's beneficiaries; and
  - preparing a final accounting of the estate/closed probate administration.

Durable Power of Attorney

- A written document authorizing a party to act on behalf of the person granting the power of attorney when the principal becomes incapacitated.

Health Care Surrogate

- A document designating a party to make all health care decisions during any period of incapacity.

Living Will

- The purpose of the living will is to direct the provision, the withholding or withdrawal of life prolonging procedures in the event one should have a terminal condition.